SOUS VIDE

COOKBOOK 2021

Modern And Most Delicious Sous Vide Recipes

Elena Kyle

TABLE OF CONTENTS

INTRODUCTION

This cookbook will help you mastering the technique of Sous Vide. In fact, most, if not all of the top restaurants around the world tend to use this technique to elevate their meals to the next level.

From fast-foods to the British Royal Navy! All of them utilize this technique to get the perfect meal every single time.

Just in case you are wondering, there is no secret "magical" spell behind all of these. It's a simple matter of consistent heating.

Ever since the olden days, human beings have tried to control and tame the powers of heat for braising, sealing, roasting, keeping them warm and, of course, cooking!

Thanks to the desire of Man to control the power of fire, culinary evolutions have given birth to the stove, ovens and even the very simple yet useful temperature dials!

And it is, throughout these steps of innovation, that the honorable method of Sous Vide came into existence.

The origin of Sous Vide lies in the mid 1970's when a famous chef known as Georges Praulus developed the technique simply as a means of trying to minimize costly shrinkage, and create an optimal environment for cooking the extremely luxurious foie gras.

Later on, this technique was enhanced by Chef Bruno Goussault who adopted this technique and started to cater to the first-class travelers of Air France by creating meals that simply left them spellbound.

SEAFOOD

1. Crispy Catfish Fingers

Preparation time: 10 minutes Cooking time: 10 minutes Servings: 4

Ingredients:

- 1 1/2 pound catfish fillets
- 3 cups canola oil
- 1 cup cornmeal
- 1/4 cup cayenne pepper
- Salt as per taste

Directions:

1. Take a mixing bowl and toss the catfish with salt and cayenne pepper.
2. Set the sous vide machine to 195 degrees Fahrenheit.
3. Take the catfish fillets in a ziplock bag. Seal it.
4. Place this bag in the water bath for 5 minutes.
5. Spread the cornmeal in a place and keep aside.
6. Coat the fish with cornmeal and fry them in oil at 350 degrees Fahrenheit until golden.

7. Transfer it to a baking sheet pat to remove excess oil.

8. Serve hot.

Nutrition:

calories 460kcal, fats 28g, protein 45g.

POULTRY

2. Extra Spicy Habanero Chicken Wings

Preparation Time: 15 minutes Cooking Time: 4 hours 15 minutes Cooking Temperature: 160°F

Ingredients:

For Sauce:

- 6 habanero peppers
- 3 tablespoons white vinegar
- 1 teaspoon butter or oil

For Wings:

- 40 split chicken wings
- Salt and freshly ground black pepper, to taste

Directions:

1. Attach the sous vide immersion circulator to a Cambro container or pot with water using an adjustable clamp and preheat water to 160°F.

2. For sauce: add all sauce ingredients in a blender and pulse until smooth. Reserve 1 tablespoon of sauce in a bowl.

3. Season chicken wings lightly with salt and black pepper.

4. In a cooking pouch, place chicken wings and all but the 1 tablespoon of reserved sauce. Seal pouch tightly after removing the excess air. Place pouch in sous vide bath and set the cooking time for 4 hours.

5. Preheat the oven broiler to high. Line a baking sheet with parchment paper.

6. Remove pouch from the sous vide bath and open carefully, removing chicken wings from pouch.

7. Arrange chicken wings onto the prepared baking sheet in a single layer. Broil for 10- 15 minutes, flipping once halfway through the cooking time.

8. Remove from oven and transfer into bowl of reserved sauce. Toss to coat well and serve immediately.

3. Classic Chicken Wings

Preparation Time: 15 minutes Cooking Time: 4 hours 15 minutes Cooking Temperature: 160°F

Ingredients:

For Sauce:

- 4 tablespoons hot sauce
- 2 tablespoons butter

For Wings:

- 40 split chicken wings
- Salt and freshly ground black pepper, to taste

Directions:

1. Attach the sous vide immersion circulator to a Cambro container or pot with water using an adjustable clamp and preheat water to 160°F.
2. For sauce: add hot sauce and butter to a bowl and mix until well combined. Reserve 1 tablespoon of all but the 1 tablespoon of reserved sauce in a separate bowl.
3. Season chicken wings lightly with salt and black pepper.
4. Place chicken wings and sauce in a cooking pouch. Seal pouch tightly after removing the excess air. Place pouch in sous vide bath and set the cooking time for 4 hours.

5. Preheat the oven broiler to high. Line a baking sheet with parchment paper.

6. Remove pouch from the sous vide bath and open carefully, removing the chicken wings from pouch.

7. Arrange chicken wings onto the prepared baking sheet in a single layer. Broil for 10- 15 minutes, flipping once halfway through the cooking time.

8. Remove from oven and transfer into bowl of reserved sauce. Toss to coat well and serve immediately.

4. Chicken Salad

Preparation Time: 20 minutes Cooking Time: 2 hours Cooking Temperature: 150°F

Ingredients:

- 2 pounds chicken breast
- 2 tarragon sprigs
- 2 garlic cloves, smashed
- Zest and juice of 1 lemon
- Kosher salt and freshly ground black pepper, to taste
- ½ cup mayonnaise
- 1 tablespoon honey
- 1 celery stalk, minced
- 1 garlic clove, minced
- ½ Serrano Chile, stemmed, seeded, and minced
- 2 tablespoons fresh tarragon leaves, minced

Directions:

1. Attach the sous vide immersion circulator to a Cambro container or pot with water using an adjustable clamp and preheat water to 150°F.

2. Place chicken breasts, tarragon sprigs, smashed garlic cloves, lemon zest, salt, and pepper in a cooking pouch. Seal pouch tightly after removing the excess air. Place pouch in sous vide

bath and set the cooking time for 2 hours.

3. Remove pouch from the sous vide bath and immediately plunge into a large bowl of ice water.

4. Once cooled completely, remove chicken breasts from pouch and transfer to a cutting board, discarding the tarragon sprigs, garlic, and lemon zest.

5. Roughly chop chicken and transfer place in a bowl. Add remaining ingredients and a little salt and black pepper and stir to combine. Serve immediately.

5. Whole Turkey

Preparation Time: 20 minutes Cooking Time: 7 hours 30 minutes Cooking Temperature: 185°F & 168°F

Ingredients:

- 8-10 pound whole turkey, rinsed
- Olive oil, as required
- 4 chicken breasts
- 4 fresh rosemary sprigs, divided
- 64 ounces chicken broth
- 2 fresh thyme sprigs
- Salt and freshly ground black pepper, to taste

Directions:

1. Before use, remove neck and giblets from turkey, reserving the turkey neck. Cover turkey & refrigerate until use.
2. Cut turkey neck and chicken breasts into pieces.
3. In a large pan, heat a little oil over medium heat and sear turkey neck and chicken breasts until browned. Add 2 rosemary sprigs and the chicken broth and bring to a boil. Skim the foam from the surface of the mixture. Reduce heat to low and simmer for

1 hour. Using a strainer, strain the liquid from the pan into a bowl, discarding the turkey neck and chicken pieces. Refrigerate the broth to chill it completely.

4. Attach the sous vide immersion circulator to a Cambro container or pot with water using an adjustable clamp and preheat water to 185°F.

5. Season turkey evenly with salt and pepper then cover both legs and neck bones with aluminum foil pieces.

6. Place turkey neck side down in a large cooking pouch. Place chilled broth and 2 thyme sprigs into the turkey cavity. Arrange 2 rosemary sprigs on the top side of the turkey. Seal pouch tightly after removing the excess air. Place pouch in sous vide bath and set the cooking time for 1 hour.

7. After 1 hour, set sous vide bath temperature to 168°F and set the cooking time for 5 hours.

8. Remove pouch from the sous vide bath and immediately plunge the pouch into a large bowl of ice water. Set aside for 30 minutes to cool.

9. Preheat conventional oven to 350°F.

10. Remove turkey from pouch, reserving cooking liquid in a pan. Transfer turkey to a roasting pan with a raised grill. Roast for 1½ hours.

For gravy:

1. place the pan of reserved cooking liquid over medium heat and simmer until desired thickness.

2. Remove turkey from oven and allow to cool on cutting board for 15-20 minutes before carving.

3. Cut turkey into pieces of the desired size and serve alongside gravy.

6. Turkey Breast With Orange Rosemary Butter

Preparation Time: 20 minutes Cooking Time: 2 hours 35 minutes Cooking Temperature: 145°F

Ingredients:

For Butter Mixture:

- ¼ cup unsalted butter, softened
- 1 tablespoon honey
- Zest of navel orange
- 1 teaspoon fresh rosemary, chopped
- ½ teaspoon salt
- ⅛ teaspoon ground black pepper
- ⅛ teaspoon red pepper flakes, crushed

For Turkey Breast:

- 2 (1½-2-pound skin-on, boneless turkey breast halves
- 1½ teaspoons kosher salt
- 2 fresh rosemary sprigs

Directions:

1. Attach the sous vide immersion circulator to a Cambro container or pot with water using an adjustable clamp

and preheat water to 14

2. For butter mixture: add all butter mixture ingredients to a small bowl and mix until well combined.

3. Gently separate skin from each turkey breast half, leaving one side of skin attached to the breast. Sprinkle each exposed breast half with kosher salt. Evenly rub butter mixture under and on top of the skin .

4. Place turkey breast halves and rosemary sprigs in a large cooking pouch. Seal pouch tightly after removing the excess air. Place pouch in sous vide bath and set the cooking time for 2½ hours.

5. Preheat the oven broiler to high.

6. Remove pouch from the sous vide bath and open carefully. Remove turkey breast halves from pouch and pat dry with paper towels. Place on a roasting tray.

7. Broil for 5 minutes.

8. Remove turkey breast halves from the oven. Cut into desired slices and serve.

7. Turkey Breast With Spiced Sage Rub

Preparation Time: 15 minutes Cooking Time: 4 hours 5 minutes Cooking Temperature: 133°F

Ingredients:

For Brine:

- 8 cups water
- 2 tablespoons light brown sugar
- ¼ cup kosher salt
- 1 teaspoon black peppercorns
- ½ teaspoon allspice berries

For Turkey:

- 1 whole skin-on, boneless turkey breast, about 4 pounds

For Rub:

- 2 tablespoons fresh sage leaves, minced
- 2 garlic cloves, minced
- 1½ teaspoon fennel seeds, crushed
- ¼ teaspoon red pepper flakes, crushed

For Searing:

- Olive oil, as required

Directions:

For brine: add all brine ingredients to a large bowl and mix until brown sugar and salt dissolve. Place turkey breast in the bowl and refrigerate, covered, for 6-8 hours.

For rub:

1. add all rub ingredients in a bowl and mix until well combined.
2. Attach the sous vide immersion circulator to a Cambro container or pot with water using an adjustable clamp and preheat water to 133°F.
3. Remove turkey breast from brine and pat dry with paper towels.
4. Arrange turkey breast on a smooth surface so that it is flat. Spread rub mixture evenly over breast. Roll up breast into a cylinder and tie with kitchen twine at 1-inch intervals.
5. Place turkey roll in a cooking pouch. Seal pouch tightly after removing the excess air. Place pouch in sous vide bath and set the cooking time for 4 hours.
6. Remove pouch from the sous vide bath and open carefully. Remove turkey roll from pouch and pat dry with paper towels.
7. Heat oil in a skillet. Place turkey roll skin side down in skillet and sear until browned completely.

8. Remove from heat and carefully remove kitchen twine. Cut into slices of the desired size and serve immediately.

MEAT

8. Pineapple Grilled Prime Rib Roast

Preparation Time: 10 hours 40 minutes Servings: 6

Get ready to a fork-tender meat with a perfectly chewy texture. Serve with a cooked wild rice.

Nutrition: 422 Calories; 17g Fat; 29g Carbs; 41g Protein; 18g Sugars

Ingredients

- 2 pounds prime rib roast
- 3 tablespoons olive oil
- 1 tablespoon honey
- 1 teaspoon chipotle powder
- 1 teaspoon granulated garlic
- 1 teaspoon mustard seeds
- 1/4 cup tamari sauce
- 1 (8-ounce can pineapple rings

Directions

1. Add prime rib roast to a large-sized mixing dish. Now, add the olive oil, honey, chipotle powder, granulated garlic, mustard seeds, tamari sauce, and pineapple juice; reserve the pineapple rings.

2. Let it marinate at least 30 minutes in your refrigerator. Remove the beef from the marinade.

3. Preheat a sous vide water bath to 140 degrees F.

4. Place the marinated beef in a large-sized cooking pouch and seal tightly. Submerge the cooking pouch in the water bath; cook for 10 hours.

5. Remove sous vide prime rib roast from the cooking pouch and pat dry.

6. Afterwards, finish the sous vide prime rib roast on a grill pan; cook approximately 40 seconds per side, basting with the reserved marinade. Set aside.

7. After that, place a few pineapple rings onto the grill pan; allow pineapple rings to cook until they show grill marks.

8. Serve the prime rib roast topped with the grilled pineapple rings. Bon appétit!

9. Beef Brisket with Peanut Sauce

Preparation Time: 12 hours 10 minutes Servings: 6

This rich and nutritious beef dish combines melt- in-your-mouth beef brisket with roasted peanut, Thai chilies, and herbs. Amazing!

Nutrition: 304 Calories; 25g Fat; 2g Carbs; 21g Protein; 6g Sugars

Ingredients

- 1 ½ pounds beef brisket
- Sea salt and ground black pepper, to taste
- 1 sprig fresh thyme
- 1 sprig fresh rosemary
- 2 bay leaves
- 1/2 teaspoon whole cloves
- 2 teaspoons peanut oil
- 1 shallot, diced
- 1/4 cup peanuts, roasted and salted
- 2 Thai chilies, stemmed
- 1 tablespoon fish sauce

Directions

1. Preheat a sous vide water bath to 176 degrees F.
2. Season the beef brisket with salt and pepper.
3. Place the seasoned beef brisket in a large- sized cooking pouch;

add the thyme, rosemary, bay leaves, and whole cloves; seal tightly.

4. Submerge the cooking pouch in the water bath; cook for 12 hours.

5. Heat the peanut oil in a skillet over a moderately high heat. Once hot, sear the beef brisket for 2 minutes, turning over once or twice; reserve.

6. Pulse the shallot, peanuts, and chilies in your food processor until finely chopped. Add this mixture to the preheated skillet and cook an additional minute.

7. Return the beef brisket to the pan, add fish sauce and stir for 1 to 2 minutes longer to let the flavors meld. Serve immediately.

10. Ribeye Steak with Classic Pepper Sauce

Preparation Time: 8 hours 10 minutes Servings: 6

Make sure to choose your desired doneness before you start cooking: 125 degrees F for rare; 131 degrees F for medium-rare; 140 degrees F for medium-well.

Nutrition: 344 Calories; 24g Fat; 1g Carbs; 39g Protein; 3g Sugars

Ingredients

- 2 pounds ribeye steak
- Garlic salt and freshly ground black pepper, to your liking
- 1/2 teaspoon mustard powder
- 1/2 teaspoon celery seeds
- 2 tablespoons butter, at room temperature
- 1 tablespoon mixed peppercorns
- 1 cup evaporated milk
- 1 tablespoon fish sauce
- 1/2 cup fresh cilantro, chopped

Directions

1. Preheat a sous vide water bath to 131 degrees F.
2. Season the ribeye steak with garlic salt, pepper, mustard powder, and celery seeds.
3. Place the seasoned ribeye steak in a large- sized cooking pouch

and seal tightly. Submerge the cooking pouch in the water bath; cook for 8 hours.

4. Melt the butter in a cast-iron pan that is preheated over a moderately high heat. Sear the steak for a minute or two on each side.

5. Turn down heat to simmer; add the peppercorns and milk to the pan. Allow it to simmer approximately 2 minutes

6. Add the fish sauce, and continue to simmer stirring constantly, until the sauce is slightly thickened.

7. Spoon the sauce over ribeye steak, garnish with fresh cilantro and enjoy!

11. Hungarian Beef Stew

Preparation Time: 18 hours 10 minutes Servings: 6

Here's a recipe for scrumptious family stew you'll never want to be without. Serve with a dollop of sour cream, mashed sweet potatoes or coleslaw.

Nutrition: 312 Calories; 17g Fat; 2g Carbs; 33g Protein; 9g Sugars

Ingredients

- 3 slices bacon
- 2 pounds stew meat, cubed
- Salt and ground black pepper, to taste
- 1 tablespoon Hungarian paprika
- 1 ½ tablespoons all-purpose flour
- 2 parsnips, chopped
- 2 carrots, chopped
- 2 shallots, peeled and chopped
- 2 red bell peppers, sliced
- 3 cloves garlic, smashed
- 3 cups broth, preferably homemade
- 2 tablespoons ketchup
- 2 bay leaves

Directions

1. Preheat a sous vide water bath to 165 degrees F.

2. Heat a pan over medium flame. Cook the bacon, stirring periodically, until it is crisp, about 7 minutes; reserve.

3. Pat the stew meat dry with paper towels; coat the meat cubes on all sides with the salt, black pepper, Hungarian paprika, and all-purpose flour.

4. Then, sear the seasoned meat until browned, working in batches; reserve.

5. Now, heat the pan over a moderate heat. Cook the parsnips, carrots, shallots, and pepper for about 8 minutes.

6. Stir in the garlic and cook until fragrant. Place the reserved bacon, meat, and vegetables in cooking pouches. Add the remaining ingredients and seal tightly.

7. Submerge the cooking pouches in the water bath; cook for 18 hours.

8. Serve in individual soup bowls and enjoy!

12. Rich Family Beef Soup

Preparation Time: 18 hours 40 minutes Servings: 6

This recipe might go on your list of favorite weekend meals. Root vegetables create a burst of flavor!

Nutrition: 425 Calories; 13g Fat; 38g Carbs; 49g Protein; 8g Sugars

Ingredients

- 1 ½ pounds boneless chuck roast, cut into 2-inch pieces
- Sea salt and ground black pepper, to taste
- 1 tablespoon tallow
- 1 leek, sliced
- 2 parsnips, sliced
- 2 carrots, sliced
- 2 celery stalks, diced
- 2 garlic cloves, minced
- 2 ripe tomatoes, chopped
- 2 bay leaves
- 6 cups broth, preferably homemade
- 3 tablespoons bouillon granules
- 1 pound turnips. chopped
- 1 pound potatoes, chopped
- 1 tablespoon balsamic vinegar

Directions

1. Preheat a sous vide water bath to 165 degrees F.

2. Season the chuck roast liberally with salt and black pepper.

3. Place the seasoned beef in a large-sized cooking pouch and seal tightly. Submerge the cooking pouch in the water bath; cook for 18 hours.

4. Remove the beef from the cooking pouch, reserving the cooking liquid.

5. Melt the tallow in a stockpot over a moderately high flame. Sear the beef for 1 minute, stirring periodically; reserve.

6. In the same pan, sauté the leeks until tender; add the parsnip, carrot, and celery and cook until softened.

7. Now, stir in the garlic, chopped tomatoes, and bay leaves; cook an additional 1 to 2 minutes.

8. Add the broth and bouillon granules, bringing it to a boil. Add the remaining ingredients, including the reserved beef.

9. Turn down heat to simmer. Cover with the lid and continue cooking for a further 30 minutes.

10. Ladle into individual serving bowls and serve hot. Bon appétit!

13. Filet De Boeuf En Croute

Preparation Time: 4 hours 15 minutes Servings: 6

Looking for a festive Christmas dinner idea? This recipe is so addictive, you will make it year after year. Serve with pickles and a decadent sauce of your choice.

Nutrition: 323 Calories; 29g Fat; 13g Carbs; 12g Protein; 3g Sugars

Ingredients

- 2 filet mignon steaks, 2-inch thick
- Sea salt and ground black pepper, to taste
- 1 teaspoon mustard powder
- 1 tablespoon olive oil
- 2 cloves garlic, chopped
- 1 sheet puff pastry, thawed
- 4 thick slices Muenster cheese
- 1 whole egg
- 2 teaspoons milk

Directions

1. Preheat a sous vide water bath to 140 degrees F.
2. Season the filet mignon with salt, black pepper, and mustard powder.
3. Place the seasoned filet mignon in a large- sized cooking pouch

and seal tightly. Submerge the cooking pouch in the water bath; cook for 3 hours.

4. Remove the beef from the cooking pouch, reserving the cooking liquid.

5. Heat the olive oil in a skillet that is preheated over a moderately high heat. Sear the filet mignon with garlic for 1 to 2 minutes.

6. Roll out puff pastry and cut it in half.

7. Add the seared filet mignon. Place the slices of cheese onto center of pastry sheets; fold pastry over.

8. In a small mixing dish, make the egg wash by whisking the egg and milk. Brush the pastry sheets with the egg wash.

9. Prick top of the pastry with a fork; cover with plastic wrap, and let it chill for 1 hour in your refrigerator.

10. Bake at 470 degrees F for about 8 to 12 minutes. Serve immediately.

14. Marinated and Grilled Flank Steak

Preparation Time: 16 hours 10 minutes Servings: 4

This recipe makes a sous vide cooking feel exciting, easy, and luxurious. Consider some add- ons such as angel hair, couscous, noodles, or green beans.

Nutrition: 348 Calories; 14g Fat; 7g Carbs; 37g Protein; 4g Sugars

Ingredients

- 1 tablespoons olive oil
- 1/4 cup red wine vinegar
- 1/4 cup soy sauce
- 2 tablespoons lime juice
- 2 tablespoons soy sauce
- 2 cloves garlic, minced
- 1 tablespoon Dijon mustard
- Salt and ground black pepper, to taste
- 1 teaspoon paprika
- 1 ½ pounds flank steak

Directions

1. In a mixing bowl, thoroughly combine the olive oil, wine vinegar, soy sauce, lime juice, soy sauce, garlic, mustard, salt, black pepper, and paprika.

2. Add the flank steak and let it marinate for 4 hours.

3. Preheat a sous vide water bath to 140 degrees F.

4. Place the marinated flank steak in a large- sized cooking pouch and seal tightly. Submerge the cooking pouch in the water bath; cook for 12 hours.

5. Remove the flank steak from the cooking pouch, reserving the cooking liquid.

6. Preheat your grill to medium-high heat. Place the steaks on the grill. Grill the flank steak for 3 to 4 minutes per side, basting with the reserved marinade. Serve immediately.

15. Blade Steaks with Champagne-Butter Sauce

Preparation Time: 10 hours 10 minutes Servings: 6

This recipe may sound fancy-schmancy but it is so easy to make by using sous vide technique. Make for any occasion and your guest will be amazed.

Nutrition: 467 Calories; 39g Fat; 3g Carbs; 45g Protein; 5g Sugars

Ingredients

- 2 pounds blade steaks
- Salt and ground black pepper, to taste
- 1 tablespoon peanut oil
- 1/2 cup butter
- 2 rosemary sprigs, chopped
- 2 thyme sprigs, chopped
- 3 garlic cloves, minced
- 1/4 cup Champagne wine

Directions

1. Preheat a sous vide water bath to 140 degrees F.
2. Sprinkle blade steaks with the salt and ground black pepper.
3. Place the seasoned flank steak in a large- sized cooking pouch and seal tightly. Submerge the cooking pouch in

the water bath; cook for 10 hours.

4. Heat the oil in a skillet over medium-high heat. Once hot, sear the steaks on all sides until well browned; set aside.

5. Melt the butter in the same skillet over moderate heat. Add the rosemary, thyme, and garlic; cook until they are aromatic.

6. Remove from heat and add Champagne wine. Spoon the sauce over the prepared steaks and serve. Bon appétit!

16. Hot Peppery Pot Roast

Preparation Time: 12 hours 10 minutes Servings: 4

Mix the seasonings, ketchup, honey, and red wine for an incredibly tasty sauce. Served with a hot barley and crispy lettuce, this pot roast recipe would win your heart!

Nutrition: 337 Calories; 8g Fat; 17g Carbs; 57g Protein; 13g Sugars

Ingredients

- 1 ½ pounds pot roast, cubed
- Salt and ground black pepper
- 1 medium-sized leek, chopped
- 2 bell peppers, deveined and sliced
- 1 serrano pepper, deveined and sliced
- 3 carrots, cut into 2-inch pieces
- 1/2 cup red wine
- 1/2 teaspoon allspice
- 1/2 teaspoon onion powder
- 1/2 teaspoon garlic powder
- 1 tablespoons honey
- 2 tablespoons ketchup
- 1/2 cup broth, preferably homemade
- 2 sprigs fresh rosemary

Directions

1. Preheat a sous vide water bath to 156 degrees F.

2. Season the pot roast with salt and black pepper.

3. Place the seasoned pot roast in cooking pouches and seal tightly. Submerge the cooking pouches in the water bath; cook for 12 hours.

4. Remove the pot roast from the cooking pouch, reserving the cooking liquid.

5. Heat the oil in a pan; sear the beef for a minute or so, working in batches. Reserve.

6. Then, in the same pan, sauté the leeks, peppers, and carrots until just tender.

7. Add the wine to deglaze the pot. Add the remaining ingredients and continue cooking until the sauce has reduced slightly.

8. Return the meat back to the pan, stir and serve!

17. Shoulder Steak in Cider Sauce

Preparation Time: 24 hours 10 minutes Servings: 4

You can add any additional herbs or aromatics you like. You can also add a few strips of bacon to the pan and skip the olive oil.

Nutrition: 314 Calories; 17g Fat; 19g Carbs; 35g Protein; 3g Sugars

Ingredients

- 1 ½ pounds shoulder steak
- Sea salt, to taste
- 1/4 teaspoon ground black pepper
- 1/2 teaspoon dried basil
- 1/2 teaspoon dried rosemary
- 1/2 teaspoon cayenne pepper
- 1 tablespoon olive oil
- 2 carrots, sliced
- 1 parsnip, sliced
- 2 leeks, thinly sliced
- 2 garlic cloves, minced
- 1/3 cup broth, preferably homemade
- 1/2 cup pear cider vinegar
- 2 tablespoons ketchup

Directions

1. Preheat a sous vide water bath to 140 degrees F.

2. Season the shoulder steak generously with salt, black pepper, basil, rosemary, and cayenne pepper.

3. Place the seasoned shoulder steak in cooking pouches and seal tightly. Submerge the cooking pouches in the water bath; cook for 24 hours.

4. Heat the oil in a cast-iron pan over a moderately high heat. Once hot, sear the shoulder steak for 40 seconds per side; reserve.

5. Then, in the same pan, cook the carrots, parsnip, and leeks. Cook until softened.

6. Add the remaining ingredients and cook until heated through. Return the beef back to the pan and serve over hot cooked rice. Bon appétit!

18. Perfect Beef Chili

Preparation Time: 3 hours Servings: 8

This hearty beef chili features ground chuck and a combo of traditional chili seasonings. Serve with salsa, crushed tortilla chips, or shredded cheese and enjoy!

Nutrition: 392 Calories; 16g Fat; 33g Carbs; 33g Protein; 3g Sugars

Ingredients

- 2 tablespoons grapeseed oil
- 2 pounds ground chuck roast
- 2 onions, chopped
- 1 bay leaf
- 2 garlic cloves, crushed
- 4 cups broth, preferably homemade
- 4 ripe tomatoes, chopped
- 1 teaspoon chili powder
- 1 teaspoon basil
- 1 teaspoon dried sage
- 3 (15-ounce cans dark red kidney beans

Directions

1. Preheat a sous vide water bath to 140 degrees F.
2. Heat the oil in a cast-iron skillet over a moderately high heat.

Once hot, cook the ground chuck, onions, and bay leaf for 3 to 4 minutes, stirring continuously.

3. Place this sautéed meat mixture in cooking pouches; seal tightly. Submerge the cooking pouches in the water bath; cook for 2 hours 30 minutes.

4. Add sous vide ground beef to a deep pan. Stir in the remaining ingredients and turn the heat to medium-low.

5. Allow it to simmer, covered, for 20 minutes more, or until thoroughly heated. Bon appétit!

19. Pork Chops in Creamy Vidalia Sauce

Preparation Time: 6 hours 50 minutes Servings: 4

Blade chops are cut from tougher parts of the pig. That's where sous vide comes in. Serve over hot cooked rice or your favorite pasta.

Nutrition: 386 Calories; 25g Fat; 6g Carbs; 38g Protein; 9g Sugars

Ingredients

- 1 ½ pounds pork blade chops
- 1/2 teaspoon kosher salt
- 1/2 teaspoon paprika
- 1/4 teaspoon ground black pepper
- 2 tablespoons olive oil
- 1/2 pound Vidalia onions, sliced into rings
- 1/2 cup beef stock
- 1 teaspoon mustard powder
- 6 ounces sour cream

Directions

1. Preheat a sous vide water bath to 141 degrees F.
2. Season blade chops with salt, paprika, and pepper.
3. Now, add the blade chops to cooking pouches and seal tightly. Submerge the cooking pouches in the water bath; cook for 6 hours 30 minutes.

4. Pat the chops dry with paper towels.

5. Then, heat the oil in a saucepan over a moderately high heat. Sauté Vidalia onions until they are tender and caramelized, about 6 to 7 minutes.

6. Add the beef stock and mustard powder; add the reserved pork. Reduce the heat and continue to simmer an additional 5 minutes.

7. Stir in the sour cream and continue to cook for a further 4 minutes. Serve on individual plates and enjoy!

20. Easy and Saucy Pork Sirloin Chops

Preparation Time: 5 hours 15 minutes Servings: 4

Why choose either moist but with no crust or crispy but dry pork chops? As a matter of fact, you can have it all!

Nutrition: 386 Calories; 25g Fat; 6g Carbs; 38g Protein; 9g Sugars

Ingredients

- 1 ½ pounds pork sirloin chops
- 1/2 teaspoon salt
- 1/4 teaspoon freshly ground black pepper
- 1/2 teaspoon cayenne pepper
- 1/2 teaspoon dried oregano
- 1 teaspoon dried basil
- 1 teaspoon smashed garlic
- 1/2 cup broth, preferably homemade
- 2 tablespoons olive oil
- 1 cup leeks, chopped
- 2 bell pepper, seeded and chopped

Directions

1. Preheat a sous vide water bath to 140 degrees F.
2. Now, season pork sirloin chops with salt, black pepper, cayenne pepper, oregano, basil, and garlic.

3. After that, add the pork sirloin chops and broth to cooking pouches and seal tightly. Submerge the cooking pouches in the water bath; cook for 8 hours.

4. Pat the pork chops dry with paper towels, reserving the cooking liquid.

5. Heat the oil in a skillet that is preheated over a moderately high heat. Sear the pork sirloin chops for 3 minutes per side; reserve.

6. Then, sauté the leeks and peppers in pan drippings until they are tender; add a splash of reserved cooking liquid.

7. Now, cook until the sauce has thickened slightly; add the reserved pork chops. Serve immediately. Bon appétit!

VEGETABLES

21. Infused Pineapple With Sorbet

Preparation time: 20 minutes Cooking time: 1 hour Servings: 6

Ingredients:

Pineapple:

- 1 pineapple, peeled, cored, and cut into 6 rectangles
- 2 cups sugar
- 10 pink peppercorns
- 1-star anise

Sorbet:

- 2 cups passion fruit puree
- 2 large bananas
- 1 ½ cups water
- 1 cup sugar
- 2 tablespoons orange juice

Method:

1. Preheat your Sous vide cooker to 149F.
2. Add sugar in a saucepan with a hint of water. Heat until

the sugar is dissolved and turns brown.

3. Pour the caramel over the pineapple.

4. Once the pineapple is cooled, transfer it to sous vide bag. Add the peppercorns and anise. Vacuum seal the bag and submerge in water.

5. Cook the pineapple 60 minutes.

Finishing steps:

1. While the pineapple is cooking, make the sorbet. Blend all ingredients in a food blender.

2. Strain and churn into ice cream making a machine, or freeze 4 hours.

3. Remove the pineapple from the bag and serve with passionfruit sorbet.

Nutrition:

Calories 405 Total Fat 8g Total Carb 138g Dietary Fiber 18g Protein 6g

22. Vanilla Poached Peaches

Preparation time: 15 minutes Cooking time: 1 hour Servings: 4

Ingredients:

- 4 peaches, halved, stone removed
- ½ cup white rum
- ¾ cup brown sugar
- 2 tablespoons lemon juice
- ½ vanilla bean, seeds scraped
- ¼ cup Greek yogurt
- 2 tablespoons honey
- ¼ cup chopped pistachios

Method:

1. Heat Sous Vide cooker to 165F.
2. In a Sous Vide bag, combine peaches, rum, ¼ cup brown sugar, lemon juice, and vanilla.
3. Vacuum seal the bag and cook the peaches in the cooker for 1 hour.

Finishing steps:

1. In a small bowl, combine Greek yogurt and honey.
2. Open the bag and pour the poaching liquid into a saucepan. Add brown sugar and simmer 6-7 minutes or until thickened.

3. Serve peaches on a plate. Fill the cavities with Greek yogurt and drizzle all with the syrup.

4. Serve.

Nutrition:

Calories 290 Total Fat 5g Total Carb 51g Dietary Fiber 7g Protein 5g

23. Plums In Red Wine

Preparation time: 5 minutes Cooking time: 30 minutes Servings: 2

Ingredients:

- 4 large plums
- 1 cup quality red wine
- ½ cup granulated sugar
- 1 teaspoon lime zest
- ½ vanilla seed pod

Method:

1. Preheat Sous Vide cooker to 170F.
2. Cut the plums in half and remove the stone.
3. Place the plums, wine, sugar, lime zest, and vanilla into Sous Vide bag.
4. Vacuum seal the bag and cook 30 minutes.

Finishing steps:

1. Open the bag and pour the cooking liquid into a plastic container.
2. Freeze the cooking liquid.

3. Serve the plums on a plate.

4. Scrub the poaching liquid with a fork and serve with plums.

Nutrition:

Calories 323 Total Fat 4g Total Carb 65g Dietary Fiber 9g Protein 1g

24. Orange Compote

Preparation time: 10 minutes Cooking time: 3 hours Servings: 4

Ingredients:

- 4 blood oranges, quartered and thinly sliced
- 2 cups granulated sugar
- 1 lemon, juice and zest
- ½ vanilla seed pod
- 1 teaspoon beef gelatin powder or agar agar

Method:

1. Set the Sous Vide cooker to 190F.
2. Combine all ingredients in a Sous Vide bag.
3. Seal using water immersion technique.
4. Cook the oranges 3 hours.

Finishing steps:

1. Remove the bag from the cooker and place into an ice-cold water bath.
2. Once cooled transfer into a food processor.
3. Add the gelatin and process until smooth.

4. Allow cooling completely before serving.

Nutrition:

Calories 466 Total Fat 3g Total Carb 121g Dietary Fiber 9g Protein 9g

25. Lime Artichokes

Preparation time: 5 minutes Cooking time: 35 minutes Servings: 4

Ingredients:

- 4 artichokes, trimmed and halved
- 1 tablespoon lime juice
- 2 tablespoons balsamic vinegar
- ½ teaspoon coriander, ground
- A pinch of salt and black pepper

Directions:

In a large sous vide bag, mix the artichokes with the lime juice and the other ingredients, seal the bag, submerge in the water bath, cook at 160 degrees F for 35 minutes, divide between plates and serve.

Nutrition:

calories 56, fat 8, fiber 4, carbs 5, protein 6

26. Basil Green Beans

Preparation time: 10 minutes Cooking time: 35 minutes Servings: 4

Ingredients:

- 1 pound green beans, trimmed
- 1 tablespoon soy sauce
- 1 tablespoon butter, melted
- Juice of ½ lime
- 2 tablespoons basil, chopped
- A pinch of salt and black pepper
- A pinch of red pepper flakes
- A pinch of salt and black pepper

Directions:

In a sous vide bag, mix the green beans with the soy sauce, butter and the other ingredients, seal the bag, submerge in the water bath, cook at 174 degrees F for 35 minutes, divide the between plates and serve.

Nutrition:

calories 10, fat 1, fiber 8, carbs 6, protein 6

27. Buttery Leeks

Preparation time: 5 minutes Cooking time: 25 minutes Servings: 4

Ingredients:

- 2 leeks, sliced
- 2 tablespoons lime juice
- 2 tablespoons butter, melted
- 1 tablespoon dill, chopped
- ½ teaspoon coriander, ground
- A pinch of salt and black pepper

Directions:

In a sous vide bag, mix the leeks with the melted butter and the other ingredients, seal the bag, submerge in the water oven, cook at 170 degrees F for 25 minutes, divide the mix between plates and serve.

Nutrition:

calories 148, fat 8, fiber 9, carbs 4, protein 5

28. Green Beans and Capers

Preparation time: 5 minutes Cooking time: 30 minutes Servings: 4

Ingredients:

- 1 pound green beans, trimmed and halved
- 1 tablespoon balsamic vinegar
- ½ teaspoon chili powder
- Juice of ½ lemon
- 1 tablespoon capers, drained
- 1 tablespoon sweet paprika
- 1 tablespoon basil, chopped
- 2 garlic cloves, chopped

Directions:

In a sous vide bag, mix the green beans with the capers, vinegar and the other ingredients, seal the bag, submerge in the water bath, cook at 164 degrees F for 30 minutes, divide the mix between plates, and serve.

Nutrition:

calories 106, fat 9, fiber 2, carbs 5, protein 8

29. Balsamic Tomatoes

Preparation time: 5 minutes Cooking time: 30 minutes Servings: 4

Ingredients:

- 1 pound cherry tomatoes, halved
- 2 tablespoons balsamic vinegar
- 2 tablespoons avocado oil
- 1 tablespoon basil, chopped
- ½ teaspoon chili powder
- ½ teaspoon sweet paprika
- A pinch of salt and black pepper
- 1 tablespoon chives, chopped

Directions:

In a sous vide bag, mix the tomatoes with the vinegar, oil and the other ingredients, seal the bag, submerge in the water bath, cook at 167 degrees F for 30 minutes, divide mix between plates and serve.

Nutrition:

calories 42, fat 2, fiber 7, carbs 1, protein 5

SNACKS

30. Chicken Stew with Mushrooms

Preparation time: 20 minutes Cooking Time: 50 minutes; Servings: 2

Nutrition:

Calories: 242 Total Fat: 8 Saturated Fat: 1g Trans Fat: 0g Protein: 33g

Ingredients:

- 2 medium-sized chicken thighs, skinless
- ½ cup fire-roasted tomatoes, diced
- ½ cup chicken stock
- 1 tablespoon tomato paste
- ½ cup button mushrooms, chopped
- 1 medium-sized celery stalk
- 1 small carrot, chopped
- 1 small onion, chopped
- 1 tablespoon dried basil, finely chopped
- 1 garlic clove, crushed
- ½ teaspoon salt
- ¼ teaspoon black pepper, ground

Serve with:

- Sour cream and basil

Directions:

1. Rinse the thighs and remove the skin. Rub with salt and pepper. Set aside.
2. Clean the vegetables. Peel and chop the onion, slice the carrot. Chop the celery stalk into half-inch long pieces.
3. Now place the meat in a large Ziploc bag along with onion, carrot, mushrooms, celery stalk, and fire roasted tomatoes. Cook en sous vide for 45 minutes at
4. Remove from the water bath and open the bag. The meat should be falling off the bone easily, so remove the bones.
5. Heat up some oil in a medium-sized saucepan and add garlic. Briefly fry – for about 3 minutes, stirring constantly. Now add chicken along with cooked vegetables, chicken stock, tomato paste, and basil. Bring it to a boil and reduce the heat to medium.
6. Cook for five more minutes, stirring occasionally.

31. Zucchini Beef Stew

Preparation time: 25 minutes Cooking Time: 6 hours; Servings: 4

Nutrition:

Calories: 383 Total Fat: 15g Saturated Fat: 14g Trans Fat: 0g Protein: 53g

Ingredients:

- 1 pound lean ground beef
- ½ cup button mushrooms, sliced
- 3 garlic cloves, crushed
- 1 cup stew beef, chopped into bite-sized pieces
- 1 small zucchini, peeled and chopped
- 1 small onion, chopped
- 1 cup tomato sauce
- 1 small carrot, chopped
- 2 cups beef broth
- 1 tablespoon extra-virgin olive oil
- ½ tablespoon cumin, ground
- 1 teaspoon salt
- ¼ teaspoon black pepper, ground

Serve with:

- Steamed kale

Directions:

1. In a large skillet, heat up the oil over medium high heat. Add chopped onion and stir-fry until translucent. Now add ground beef and continue to cook for ten more minutes, stirring a couple of times. Remove from the heat and set aside.

2. Place stew beef in a large colander and rinse well. Season with salt and pepper and transfer to a large Ziploc bag along with mushrooms, chopped zucchini, tomato sauce, carrot, and broth.

3. Seal the bag and cook en sous vide for six hours at 140 degrees.

32. Marinara Shrimp

Preparation time: 60 minutes Cooking Time: 45 minutes; Servings: 3

Nutrition:

Calories: 362 Total Fat: 17g Saturated Fat: 2g Trans Fat: 0g Protein: 34g

Ingredients:

- 1 pound shrimps, peeled and deveined
- 1 cup tomatoes, diced
- 1/3 cup tomato paste
- ¼ cup extra virgin olive oil
- 2 tablespoon fresh parsley, finely chopped
- ½ teaspoon sea salt
- ¼ teaspoon dried oregano, ground
- ½ teaspoon dried basil, ground
- ¼ teaspoon black pepper, ground

Serve with:

- Braised chard

Directions:

1. Soak shrimps in a large pot of salted water and set aside for 30 minutes. Now clean and peel each shrimp and transfer to a large bowl. Stir in olive oil, parsley, salt, oregano, basil, and

pepper.

2. Mix well to combine and transfer to a large Ziploc along with the marinade. Cook en sous vide for 40 minutes at 131 degrees.

3. Remove from the water bath and transfer to a deep, heavy-bottomed pot. Preheat over medium-high heat and add diced tomatoes and tomato paste. Cook for 4 minutes, stirring constantly and remove from the heat.

4. Serve warm with braised chard.

33. Mediterranean Trout en Sous Vide

Preparation time: 15 minutes Cooking Time: 1 hour; Servings: 4

Nutrition:

Calories: 666 Total Fat: 61g Saturated Fat: 9g Trans Fat: 0g Protein: 38g

Ingredients:

- 1 pound trout fillet
- 1 cup extra-virgin olive oil
- 1 medium-sized lemon
- 1 large red onion, peeled and finely chopped
- 3 garlic cloves, crushed
- 2 tablespoons fresh parsley, finely chopped
- ½ teaspoon sea salt
- ¼ teaspoon black pepper, ground

Serve with:

- Steamed spinach and fresh lemon wedges

Directions:

1. Rinse and clean the fish. Using a sharp knife, gently remove the bones and cut fillets. This can be a bit tricky, so you can simply buy trout fillets.

2. Now combine olive oil with garlic, parsley, salt, and

pepper. Brush each fillet with this mixture and place in a large Ziploc. Seal the bag and cook en sous vide for one hour at 104 degrees. You want them nice and tender.

3. Remove from the Ziploc and set aside.

4. Heat up two tablespoons of olive oil in a large, non-stick grill pan. Stir-fry the onions and add fillets. Briefly fry for two minutes on each side and remove from the heat.

5. Serve with steamed spinach and lemon wedges.

DESSERTS & DRINKS

34. Honey & Citrus Apricots

Preparation Time: 70 minutes Servings: 4

Ingredients

- 6 apricots, pitted and quartered
- ½ cup honey
- 2 tbsp water
- 1 tbsp lime juice
- 1 vanilla bean pod, halved
- 1 cinnamon stick

Directions

1. Prepare a water bath and place the Sous Vide in it. Set to 179 F.

2. Place all the ingredients in a vacuum- sealable bag. Release air by the water displacement method, seal and submerge the bag in the water bath. Cook for 45 minutes. Once the timer has stopped, remove the bag and discard the vanilla bean pod and cinnamon stick. Serve right away.

35. Orange Pots du Créme with Chocolate

Preparation Time: 65 minutes + 5 hours Servings: 6

Ingredients

- ⅔ cup chopped chocolate
- 6 egg yolks
- 1⅓ cups fine white sugar
- 3 cups half and half
- 1 tsp vanilla extract
- Zest of 1 large orange
- ⅛ tsp orange extract
- 2 tbsp orange juice
- 2 tbsp chocolate-flavored liqueur

Directions

1. Prepare a water bath and place the Sous Vide in it. Set to 196 F.
2. Whit an electric mixer, combine the egg yolks and sugar. Mix for 1-2 minutes until creamy. Heat the cream in a saucepan over medium heat and add the vanilla, orange zest and extract. Cook in low heat for 3-4 minutes. Set aside and allow to cool for 2-3 minutes.
3. Melt the chocolate in the microwave. Once the mixture has cooled, pour the cream mixture into the egg mixture and stir.

Add the melted chocolate and stir until combined. Add in orange juice and chocolate liqueur. Pour the chocolate mixture into mason jars. Seal with a lid and submerge the jars in the water bath, Cook for 45 minutes. Once the timer has stopped, remove the jars and allow to cool for 5 minutes.

36. Lemon-Sage Apricots

Preparation Time: 70 minutes Servings: 4

Ingredients

- ½ cup honey
- 8 apricots, pitted and quartered
- 2 tbsp water
- 1 tbsp lemon juice
- 3 fresh sage sprigs
- 1 fresh parsley sprig

Directions

Prepare a water bath and place the Sous Vide in it. Set to 179 F. Place all the ingredients in a vacuum- sealable bag. Release air by the water displacement method, seal and submerge the bag in the water bath. Cook for 45 minutes. Once the timer has stopped, remove the bag and discard the herb springs.

37. Apple Pie

Preparation Time: 85 minutes Servings: 8

Ingredients:

- 1 pound apples, peel and cubed
- 6 ounces puff pastry
- 1 egg yolk, whisked
- 4 tbsp sugar
- 2 tbsp lemon juice
- 1 tbsp cornstarch
- 1 tsp ground ginger
- 2 tbsp butter, melted
- ¼ tsp nutmeg
- ¼ tsp cinnamon

Directions:

1. Preheat your oven to 365 F. Roll the pastry into a circle. Brush it with the butter and place in the oven. Cook for 15 minutes.

2. Prepare a water bath and place Sous Vide in it. Set to 160 F. Combine all the remaining ingredients in a vacumm-sealable bag. Release air by water displacement method,

seal and submerge in water bath. Cook for 45 minutes. Once the timer has stopped, remove the bag. Top the cooked pie crust with the apple mixture. Return to the oven and cook for 15 more minutes.

COCKTAILS AND INFUSIONS

38. Flourless Chocolate Cake

Preparation Time: 15 mins Cooking Time: 1 hour 15 mins Cooking Temperature: 115 & 170°F

Ingredients:

- ½ pound semisweet chocolate squares, chopped
- ⅛ cup coffee liqueur or orange liqueur
- 4 ounces butter
- 4 large eggs
- 2 tablespoons unsweetened cocoa powder

Directions:

1. Attach the sous vide immersion circulator using an adjustable clamp to a Cambro container or pot filled with water and preheat to 115°F.
2. Into a cooking pouch, add chocolate, coffee and butter. Seal pouch tightly after squeezing out the excess air. Place pouch in sous vide bath and set the cooking time for 15 minutes.
3. Remove pouch from sous vide bath every 5 minutes and, with your fingers, massage the mixture to mix.
4. Remove pouch from sous vide bath and carefully open it.

5. Set sous vide bath to 170°F. Generously grease 6 x 4-ounce canning jars with nonstick spray.

6. Into a bowl add eggs and, with a standing mixer, beat at high speed until volume doubles.

7. Slowly add chocolate mixture, beating on low speed until well-combined.

8. Transfer mixture evenly into prepared jars and smooth the surface by tapping each jar on the palm of your hand.

9. Close the canning jar lids tightly. Carefully arrange jars into sous vide bath and set the cooking time for 60 minutes.

10. Carefully, remove jars from sous vide bath and place onto a wire rack to cool. After cooling, refrigerate covered for at least 6 hours.

11. About 30 minutes before serving, carefully run a thin knife around the edge of each cake to remove from jars.

12. Serve with your desired garnishing.

39. GINGER CRÈME BRÛLÉE

Preparation Time: 15 mins Cooking Time: 55 mins Cooking Temperature: 185°F

Ingredients:

- ⅔ cup whole milk
- 2 cups heavy whipping cream
- 4 teaspoons peeled and fresh chopped ginger
- 4 large egg yolks
- ½ cup superfine sugar
- pinch of salt

Directions:

1. Attach the sous vide immersion circulator using an adjustable clamp to a Cambro container or pot filled with water and preheat to 185°F.
2. Into a medium pan add milk, cream and ginger, and warm through on a low heat.
3. Remove from heat and allow liquid to steep for 30 minutes.
4. Through a fine mesh sieve, strain the mixture and discard the solids.
5. Return the liquid to another pan and cook until just heated.

6. Into a bowl, add egg yolks and beat well.

7. Slowly add sugar and salt, beating continuously.

8. Slowly add ginger mixture, beating continuously until well-combined.

9. Place ⅔ cup of mixture into each ramekin. With a piece of plastic wrap, cover each ramekin and secure with a rubber band.

10. Carefully arrange ramekins over the rack in sous vide bath (water level should come ⅔ up the sides of the ramekins. Set the cooking time for 50 minutes.

11. Carefully, remove ramekins from sous vide bath onto wire rack to cool slightly.

12. Remove plastic wrap and keep aside to cool completely.

13. After cooling, refrigerate until chilled.

14. Before serving, spread a thin layer of sugar on top of each chilled custard. With a torch, caramelize top of each custard.

15. Serve immediately.

40. Flan Custard

Preparation Time: 15 mins Cooking Time: 2 hours Cooking Temperature: 180°F

Ingredients:

- ¾ cup granulated sugar
- 1 x 14-ounce can condensed milk
- 1 x 12-fluid-ounce can evaporated milk
- 12 large egg yolks
- 1 teaspoon pure vanilla extract

Directions:

1. Attach the sous vide immersion circulator using an adjustable clamp to a Cambro container or pot filled with water and preheat to 180°F.
2. Into a pan, add sugar and heat until liquefied completely. Pour liquefied sugar evenly into 4 x ½-pint jars and keep aside to cool.
3. Into a bowl, add condensed milk, evaporated milk, egg yolks and vanilla extract, and gently stir to combine.
4. Through a cheesecloth, strain mixture.
5. Pour strained mixture over liquefied sugar in each jar, leaving just enough room for the lid to close tightly.
6. Carefully arrange ramekins over the rack in sous vide bath. Set the cooking time for 2 hours.

7. Carefully, remove ramekins from sous vide bath. Place ramekins onto wire rack to cool completely.

8. After cooling, refrigerate to chill before serving.

41. Chocolate Zabaglione

Preparation Time: 15 mins Cooking Time: 30 mins Cooking Temperature: 165°F

Ingredients:

- 1 cup sugar
- ½ cup dry Marsala
- 8 large egg yolks
- pinch of salt
- ⅓ cup unsweetened cocoa powder
- ¼ cup whipping cream
- 1 pound fresh strawberries, hulled and quartered

Directions:

1. Attach the sous vide immersion circulator using an adjustable clamp to a Cambro container or pot filled with water and preheat to 165°F.
2. Into a bowl add sugar, Marsala, egg yolks and salt, and beat until well-combined.
3. Add cocoa powder and beat until well- combined.
4. Add cream and beat well.
5. Into a large cooking pouch, place egg mixture. Seal pouch tightly after squeezing out the excess air. Place pouch in sous vide bath and set the cooking time for 20- 30 minutes.

6. Remove pouch from sous vide bath occasionally and, with your fingers, massage the mixture to mix.

7. Meanwhile, divide strawberries into dessert bowls evenly.

8. Remove pouch from sous vide bath and carefully open it.

9. Place warm zabaglione over the strawberries, cover, and refrigerate to chill before serving.

42. Mexican Chocolate Pots

Preparation Time: 15 mins Cooking Time: 30 mins Cooking Temperature: 180°F

Ingredients:

- 1 x 3½-ounce bar Mexican chocolate, chopped
- 1 tablespoon sugar
- ⅓ cup whole milk
- 1 cup heavy whipping cream pus more for topping
- 3 egg yolks
- 2 teaspoons cocoa powder
- ¼ teaspoon vanilla extract
- ⅛ teaspoon sea salt
- chocolate shavings, for serving

Directions:

1. Attach the sous vide immersion circulator using an adjustable clamp to a Cambro container or pot filled with water and preheat to 180°F.

2. In a heatproof bowl, mix together chocolate and sugar. Keep aside.

3. Into a pan, add milk and cream and cook until heated completely.

4. Remove from heat and pour mixture over chocolate and sugar. Keep aside for 5 minutes.

5. Meanwhile, in another small bowl, add egg yolks, vanilla extract, cocoa powder and salt, and beat until well-combined.

6. After 5 minutes, stir the chocolate mixture until well-combined and smooth.

7. Add egg mixture and beat until well- combined.

8. Fill the ramekins evenly with chocolate mixture.

9. Arrange ramekins on a rack in the sous vide bath. (Water level should be halfway up the sides of ramekins. Using plastic wrap, cover the ramekins.

10. Set the cooking time for 30 minutes.

11. Remove from sous vide bath and keep aside for 20 minutes to cool.

12. Refrigerate for at least 2 hours before serving.

13. Top with chocolate shavings and a dollop of whipped cream, and serve.

43. Bourbon Grape & Ginger Beer Cocktail

Servings: 8 Preparation time: 30 minutes Cooking Time: 120 minutes

Ingredients

- 2-3 cups sliced seedless red grapes
- 1 ¼ cups vanilla sugar
- ½ cup bourbon
- ½ vanilla bean, split
- 1 lemon, peeled
- 1-star anise pod
- 1 cardamom pod
- ½ cup ginger beer per serving
- Fresh mint leaves
- Lemon twists
- Sliced grapes for garnishing

Directions:

1. Prepare your Sous Vide water bath using your immersion circulator and raise the temperature to 167-degrees Fahrenheit.
2. Add the grapes, sugar, vanilla, bourbon, star anise, lemon peel, and cardamom to a large resealable zip bag.
3. Seal using the immersion method and cook for 2 hours.
4. Once done, remove the bag and transfer to an ice bath,

once the grape mix is cool, transfer to the refrigerator and chill.

5. Strain the grape mixture through a metal mesh strainer over a bowl and reserve the fruit for later use.

6. Then, fill a rocks glass with ice and add ½ cup ginger beer, 1 ½ ounce of infused bourbon.

7. Garnish with mint and lemon twist.

8. Serve with a garnish of sliced grapes.

Nutrition:

Calories: 216 Carbohydrate: 23g Protein: 0g Fat: 0g Sugar: 3g Sodium: 17mg

44. Sous Vide Gin

Servings: 1 Preparation time: 10 minutes Cooking Time: 1 minute 30 seconds

Ingredients

- 3 oz. vodka
- Zest of small orange
- 8 juniper berries
- 10-12 coriander seeds
- 2 cardamom pods
- 8-10 grains of paradise
- 1 Tasmanian pepper berry

Directions:

1. Prepare your Sous Vide water bath using your immersion circulator and raise the temperature to 176-degrees Fahrenheit.
2. Add all the listed ingredients to a resealable bag and seal using the immersion method.
3. Cook for 90 seconds.
4. Once done, take the bag out from the water bath and transfer it to an ice bath.
5. Massage the bag to infuse the gin carefully.

6. Cool down the mixture and strain the mixture through a metal mesh strainer and pour it to a medium-sized bowl

7. Serve!

Nutrition:

Calories: 173 Carbohydrate: 17g Protein: 0g Fat: 0g Sugar: 16g Sodium: 14mg

45. Limoncello Vodka Cocktail

Servings: 5 Preparation time: 20 minutes Cooking Time: 180 minutes

Ingredients

- 1 bottle vodka
- Grated zest/peel of 10-15 thoroughly washed lemons
- 1 cup granulated sugar
- 1 cup water

Directions:

1. Prepare your Sous Vide water bath using your immersion circulator and raise the temperature to 135-degrees Fahrenheit.
2. Add the vodka and lemon zest to a large zip bag and seal using the immersion method. Cook for 2-3 hours.
3. Take a saucepan and put it over medium- high heat
4. Add the sugar and water and stir until the sugar dissolves to prepare the syrup
5. Once done, take the bag out from the water bath and strain through metal mesh into a bowl.
6. Stir in syrup.
7. Pour Limoncello into bottles and serve!

Nutrition:

Calories: 430 Carbohydrate: 61g Protein: 1g Fat: 0g Sugar: 53g Sodium: 8mg

46. Swedish Rosemary Snaps

Servings: 10 Preparation time: 10 minutes Cooking Time: 120 minutes

Ingredients

- 1 bottle vodka
    - 3 sprigs fresh rosemary + plus extra for storage
    - 4 strips of fresh orange peel

Directions:

1. Prepare your Sous Vide water bath using your immersion circulator and raise the temperature to 135-degrees Fahrenheit.
2. Add the vodka, 3 sprigs rosemary, and 3 strips of orange peel to a resealable zip bag.
3. Seal using the immersion method. Cook for 2 hours.
4. Once done, take the bag out from the water bath and pass through metal mesh strainer into large bowl.
5. Put one fresh sprig of rosemary and one strip of orange peel into bottle.
6. Pour the prepared snaps into bottle.
7. Chill and serve!

Nutrition:

Calories: 236 Carbohydrate: 14g Protein: 0gFat: 0g Sugar: 11g Sodium: 4mg

47. Strawberry Basil Shrub

Servings: 12 Preparation time: 10 minutes Cooking Time: 120 minutes

Ingredients

- 1 lb. fresh strawberries, trimmed
- 1 lb. ultrafine sugar
- 2 cups balsamic vinegar
- 1 cup water
- 1 cup fresh basil leaves

Directions:

1. Prepare your Sous Vide water bath using your immersion circulator and raise the temperature to 135-degrees Fahrenheit.
2. Add all the listed ingredients to a resealable zip bag.
3. Seal using the immersion method. Cook for 2 hours.
4. Once cooked, take the bag out from the water bath and pass through metal mesh strainer into large bowl.
5. Chill and serve!

Nutrition:

Calories: 150 Carbohydrate: 36g Protein: 0g Fat: 0g Sugar: 35g Sodium: 6mg

48. Drambuie

Servings: 8 Preparation time: 15 minutes Cooking Time: 30 minutes

Ingredients

- 1 cup scotch
- ½ cup water
- ½ cup honey
- 2 teaspoons fresh rosemary
- 2 teaspoons whole fennel seeds

Directions:

1. Prepare your Sous Vide water bath using your immersion circulator and raise the temperature to 180-degrees Fahrenheit.
2. Add all the above ingredients to a resealable zip bag.
3. Seal using the immersion method.
4. Cook for 30 minutes.
5. Once done, take the bag out from the water bath and pass through metal mesh strainer into a large bowl.
6. Chill and serve!

Nutrition:

Calories: 184 Carbohydrate: 24g Protein: 0g Fat: 0g Sugar: 23g Sodium: 3mg

49. Bacon Infused Bourbon

Servings: 8 Preparation time: 80 minutes Cooking Time: 60 minutes

Ingredients

- 2 cups bourbon
- 8 oz. smoked bacon, cooked until crisp
- 3 tablespoon bacon fat reserved from cooking
- 3 tablespoons light brown sugar

Directions:

1. Prepare your Sous Vide water bath using your immersion circulator and raise the temperature to 150-degrees Fahrenheit.
2. Add all the listed ingredients to a resealable zip bag.
3. Seal using the immersion method. Cook for 1 hour.
4. Once done, take the bag out from the water bath and strain the contents through a fine-mesh strainer into a large bowl
5. Transfer the bourbon to the refrigerator and chill until the pork fat solidifies on top. Skim off the fat
6. Then, strain the bourbon a second time through a cheesecloth-lined strainer.
7. Pass it to a storage container and store in the refrigerator.

Nutrition:

Calories: 274 Carbohydrate: 14g Protein: 6g Fat: 19g Sugar: 13g Sodium: 316mg

50. Lemongrass Syrup

Servings: 4 Preparation time: 15 minutes Cooking Time: 60 minutes

Ingredients

- 4 stalks lemongrass, cut into 1-inch pieces
- 1 cup water
- 1 cup ultrafine sugar

Directions:

1. Prepare your Sous Vide water bath using your immersion circulator and raise the temperature to 180-degrees Fahrenheit.
2. Add all the above ingredients to a resealable zip bag.
3. Seal using the immersion method.
4. Cook for about 1 hour.
5. Once cooked, remove the bag from the water bath and transfer it to an ice cold bath.
6. Strain into a large bowl and transfer to a container
7. Serve chilled!

Nutrition:

Calories: 208 Carbohydrate: 54g Protein: 0g Fat: 0g Sugar: 50g Sodium: 4mg

CONCLUSION

Sous vide cooking is one of the most beloved methods of cooking among five-star chefs and restauranteurs all over the world. This cooking method means

consistently delicious meals prepared quickly with the right amount of prep work. Doesn't it make sense to bring the same method to your home and family life?

We know you love your family and want the best for them. Congratulations on taking this first step in changing your family's meal quality and routine forever. Now pick your first recipe and jump right into your next favorite cooking hobby.

CPSIA information can be obtained
at www.ICGtesting.com
Printed in the USA
BVHW092324210421
605502BV00002B/250

9 781802 147346